EARLY SKILLS LIBRARY

our america

Developed by Macmillan Educational Company
Written by Marilyn LaPenta
Text illustrated by Patricia Schories
Cover illustrated by Patrick Girouard

Newbridge Educational Programs

TABLE OF CONTENTS

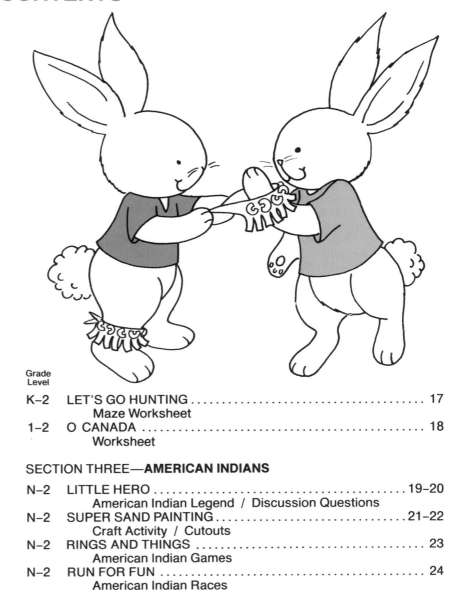

TABLE OF CONTENTS
Continued

Prepare the snacks on this page and page 6 for your class. Explain that each snack is representative of the products and traditions of a particular region of the country.

SALMON SPREAD
(Northwest)

Ingredients: one large can salmon
⅔ cup mayonnaise
two or three celery stalks
snack crackers

How to Make:

1. Empty the can of salmon into a bowl. Remove small bones.

2. Add mayonnaise and mix.

3. Wash celery stalks, remove leaves, and chop celery into small pieces. Add to the mixture and stir well.

4. Spread salmon on crackers and serve. (Makes three cups of salmon spread.)

CHEESE SNACKS
(Midwest)

Ingredients: 1 lb. sharp cheddar cheese
2 tablespoons mayonnaise
2 egg yolks
toast rounds or party bread

How to Make:

1. Cut cheese into ½" cubes and mix well with mayonnaise and egg yolks.

2. Spread on toast rounds or bread.

3. Broil in toaster oven for five minutes or until tops begin to brown. (Makes 30–40 servings.)

TEX-MEX DIP
(Southwest)

Ingredients: one 10-oz. can bean dip
ripe avocado
1 tablespoon lemon juice
½ cup sour cream
¼ cup mayonnaise
½ package taco seasoning mix
small bunch scallions
1 cup fresh tomatoes
14-oz. package shredded cheddar cheese
taco chips

How to Make:

1. Spread bean dip over the bottom of a glass pie plate.

2. Mash the avocado and mix with lemon juice. Spread on top of bean dip.

3. Mix sour cream with mayonnaise and taco seasoning, and spread on top of avocado mixture.

4. Chop scallions and sprinkle on top.

5. Chop tomatoes and sprinkle on top of scallions.

6. Sprinkle cheese on top of it all.

7. Scoop out small amounts and serve with taco chips. (Makes six cups of dip.)

BOSTON CREAM PIE
(New England)

Ingredients: yellow sponge cake mix
one box lemon or vanilla pudding mix
one square baking chocolate
1 tablespoon butter
2 tablespoons milk
1 cup powdered sugar
pinch of salt
drop of vanilla

How to Make:

1. Prepare the sponge cake, following the directions on the box.

2. Cut the sponge cake horizontally, to make two layers.

3. Prepare the lemon or vanilla pudding, following the directions on the box.

4. Spread the pudding on one layer of cake. Place the second layer on top of the pudding.

5. Prepare icing by melting the chocolate and butter in the top half of a double boiler. When melted, remove from heat and add milk, sugar, salt, and vanilla. Beat with hand mixer until smooth. Spread immediately with butter spreader over top and sides of the cake. Cool, cut, and serve. (Makes 12–16 slices.)

PECAN MUNCHIES
(South)

Ingredients: 48 vanilla wafers
2 cups chopped pecans
4 tablespoons cocoa
10 tablespoons dark corn syrup
powdered sugar

How to Make:

1. Crush wafers.

2. Stir in pecans.

3. Stir in cocoa and corn syrup.

4. Roll mixture into 1″ balls.

5. Roll balls in powdered sugar and chill overnight. (Makes three dozen munchies.)

Read this story to your class and have children complete the worksheet on page 8.

One of the most famous statues in the entire world is the Statue of Liberty. The statue was a gift of friendship from the people of France to the people of the United States.

The Statue of Liberty, or "Miss Liberty" as she is sometimes called, stands on Liberty Island in New York Harbor. She holds a lighted torch that can be seen by ships passing by. Her bright torch, held in her right hand, reminds us of our freedom. In her left hand, she holds a book that represents the Declaration of Independence. At her feet, there is a broken chain that reminds us that the United States is no longer a part of England but a free and independent country.

A Frenchman named Frédéric-Auguste Bartholdi thought of the idea for the statue. However, the statue was going to cost a great deal of money to build. So the children, farmers, shopkeepers, and workers of France decided to save as much money as they could to help build this beautiful gift. The people of the United States helped too. Schoolchildren, grocers, farmers, cowboys, and many other people raised money to build the base for the statue.

The steel framework for "Miss Liberty" was made first. Then great sheets of copper were hammered, pressed, and fitted together over the framework to make the arms, legs, fingers, and other parts of the statue. After the statue was completed in France, it was taken apart, packed in more than 200 boxes, and sent to the United States. There the pieces of the statue were put together and the statue was placed on its base. The completed statue was dedicated in 1886, 110 years after the Declaration of Independence was made.

The salty ocean air has turned "Miss Liberty's" bright copper finish green, but the freedom that the Statue of Liberty stands for is still as untarnished as it was the day she first took her place in New York Harbor.

Discussion Questions:

1. Who gave the Statue of Liberty to the United States?
2. Where does the Statue of Liberty stand?
3. What has the salty air done to the Statue of Liberty?
4. What, do you think, does the word *liberty* mean?
5. Why is the Statue of Liberty so important to Americans?

Connect the dots from A to Z to see a famous symbol of the United States.
Color the picture.

Name_____

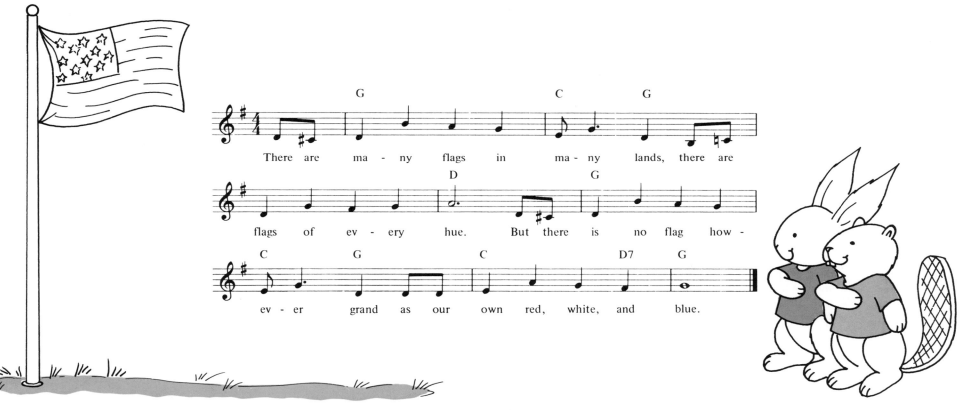

Lyrics with music:

There are ma-ny flags in ma-ny lands, there are flags of ev-ery hue. But there is no flag how-ev-er grand as our own red, white, and blue.

You need: American flag

Steps:

1. Teach the song to your class, one line at a time.

2. Display the American flag in the classroom. Explain that the words red, white, and blue in the song on this page refer to the United States flag. The Pledge of Allegiance is recited to this flag. Explain that the pledge is a promise to be loyal to the United States. The flag is the symbol that stands for the country.

3. Discuss the meaning of a promise. Ask questions such as: "Have you ever promised to do something for someone?" "What kinds of promises have you made?" "How do you feel when you keep your promise?" "How do you feel when you don't keep your promise?"

4. Choose a child to be flag bearer. The child stands in front of the class and holds the flag, facing the class. The rest of the children stand up, place their right hands over their hearts, and say the Pledge of Allegiance.

5. The children can then sing "There Are Many Flags in Many Lands." After the song, have a few children help put the flag away, either by folding it or hanging it on a pole.

Follow-up Activity:

With your class, review ways to show love and respect for the flag, such as:

a. Stand quietly when the flag is carried by.
b. Men and boys should remove their hats when they salute the flag.
c. Do not let the flag touch the ground.

Teach your class this song, one line at a time. Define words children may not know. Then make the bulletin board display shown below.

*O, beautiful for spacious skies,
For amber waves of grain,
For purple mountain majesties
Above the fruited plain,
America! America! God shed His grace on thee,
And crown thy good with brotherhood
From sea to shining sea.*

You need: 18″ × 24″ white construction paper
stapler
pencil
9″ × 12″ piece of cardboard
scissors
newspaper
blue, purple, and yellow chalk
thumbtacks
compass
paper towels
dark marker

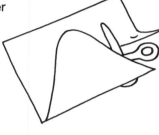

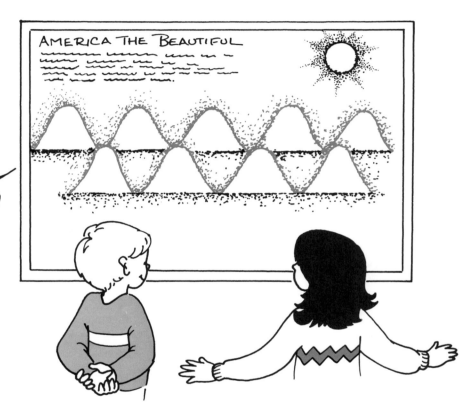

Steps:

1. Cover the bulletin board with white construction paper.

2. Draw a simple mountain outline on 9″ × 12″ cardboard, as shown, and cut it out.

3. Children take turns tracing the pattern onto white construction paper. Younger children may need help. Have children cut out the mountains.

4. Have children cover their desks with newspaper. Children will heavily chalk the top edges of their mountains blue or purple and the bottom edges of their mountains yellow.

5. Tack several chalked stencils in one row across the center of the bulletin board. Have individual children take turns using a paper towel to rub the blue and purple chalk in an upward motion onto the white paper on the bulletin board.

6. With a new paper towel, children rub the yellow chalk in a downward motion.

7. Next remove the stencils and tack several other chalked stencils in a row, slightly below the first chalked outlines. Have children repeat the rubbing process.

8. Draw and cut a 4″ circle out of white construction paper, and chalk the edges of it yellow. Tack the circle above the mountains and rub the chalk onto the bulletin board in an outward motion to create the sun's rays.

9. Use a dark marker to write the words to the song "America the Beautiful" along the top of the bulletin board.

You need: 18″ × 24″ white, red, and blue
    construction paper
    stapler
    ruler
    pencils
    scissors
    star pattern on this page
    oaktag
    photographs, postcards, or small pictures
      from magazines, of American scenes
    clear tape
    black marker

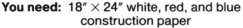

Steps:

1. Cover a large bulletin board with white construction paper.

2. Measure and cut 4″ × 24″ red construction paper strips and staple them across the bulletin board. Leave 4″-wide spaces between strips. The bulletin board will look like the United States flag, without the blue panel.

3. Reproduce the star pattern on this page and cut it out. Trace it several times onto oaktag and cut out.

4. Give each child a piece of the blue construction paper. Have each child trace the star onto it and cut it out.

5. Have children staple their stars onto the bulletin board, placing them all over.

6. Ask each child to bring in a pretty picture, photograph, or postcard of some place in the United States that he or she has visited. Encourage children to bring in pictures from as many different states as possible. Tape the picture onto the child's star. On the star, write the name of the place and the state it is in.

7. Use a black marker to write the title "All Over This Land" on blue construction paper.

8. Center the title paper and staple it onto the top of the bulletin board.

9. Let each child tell the class about his or her visit to the place shown on his or her star.

You need: 18″ × 24″ blue and white construction
paper
stapler
red marker
travel brochures, travel posters,
and picture postcards
ruler
pencil
scissors
black marker

Steps:

1. Cover the bulletin board with blue construction paper.

2. On a piece of white construction paper, write the words of the song "America the Beautiful" (see page 10), using a red marker. Staple it onto the center of the bulletin board.

3. Gather illustrated brochures and posters from your local travel agents of scenic spots in the United States. Staple these pictures onto the bulletin board around the song. Children may add their own postcards and brochures from family vacations.

4. Have a discussion with your students about the places they have visited. Focus on what they enjoyed most about each place. Suggest what some of the places would have been like if they had been littered with trash, if the water had been polluted, or if they had been too noisy.

5. Discuss how to keep America beautiful. Keep statements positive: "I will pick up after myself at the beach." "I will leave the wildflowers where they grow." "I will throw my garbage where it belongs and not in the water or on the ground."

6. Measure and cut several 2″×24″ strips of white construction paper. Choose several sentences from the children's ideas, describing what they will do to keep America beautiful. Use a black marker to write the sentences on the strips. Older children can write the sentences themselves. Staple the sentences around the bulletin board.

7. Sing "America the Beautiful" with the children.

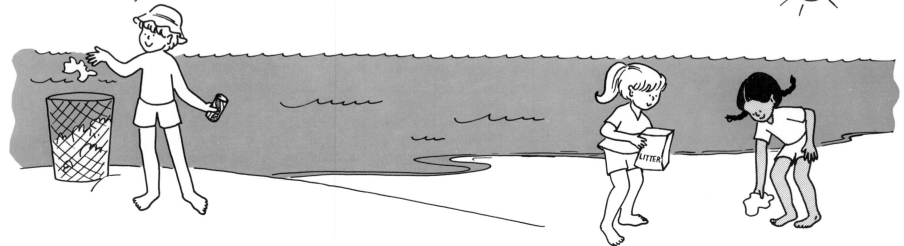

WHY THE TURNSTONES NEST NEAR THE SHORE
Inuit Legend

Read this legend to your class. Explain that Eskimos prefer to be called Inuits. Have children complete the puzzle on page 15.

Turnstones are strange-looking little birds. Their feathers appear quite black when they stand still on land. But when they fly, patches of white feathers can be seen on their wings.

Long, long ago, turnstones made their nests in the mountains of western Canada. They flew north every spring as the days grew warmer. One sunny day, as the turnstones were heading toward the mountains, an Inuit, sitting in his kayak on the ocean, saw them.

"Such lovely birds!" thought the fisherman. "They must be looking for a nesting spot." Then he went on thinking about his family and how hungry they were after the long, cold winter.

Suddenly, one turnstone flew toward his kayak. Much to the fisherman's surprise, the turnstone flew directly at him and started circling frantically around his kayak, chattering and cawing.

"How strange," thought the man. "This bird must be tired after a long trip on her way to the mountains. Maybe she wants to lay an egg, or maybe she wants to rest." So the fisherman quietly took off his cap and set it in front of the little turnstone. With a flutter, the turnstone settled right down in the cap and laid a beautiful egg.

The astonished fisherman looked at the contented bird and decided to take her in his cap to the grassy shore nearby. There he would settle the bird in a new nest. So the fisherman paddled to shore as the turnstone sat in the bow of the kayak.

The fisherman pulled his kayak onto the land and, with his cap carefully in his hand, headed toward a grassy meadow in a low, wet place. There he chose a soft spot and scooped out a little hollow just large enough for the turnstone. Gently, he placed the egg in it.

The mother turnstone seemed pleased. She twittered and chattered and fluffed her feathers, and then proudly sat down on the beautiful egg.

The fisherman, who was also pleased, went back to his kayak and paddled out to sea, hoping he still had time to catch some fish. No sooner had he lowered his net than the fish began filling it. Soon the kayak was overflowing with fish. He hurried home, and his family greeted him with great shouts of joy to see such a wonderful catch.

The next day the fisherman was amazed when he caught fish so easily again. As he paddled home, thinking about his good fortune, he decided to stop by the grassy spot where he had made the mother turnstone's nest. He peeked beneath the warm, dry grass, and the bird looked up and seemed to smile at him.

"How nice of you to come back," the bird said. "I have laid four beautiful eggs and am waiting for them to hatch."

You can imagine the fisherman's surprise when the bird spoke. He had never heard a bird talk before. After a moment, the man answered.

"I just stopped by to see if you needed anything, or if bigger birds were bothering you. They love to eat little birds' eggs."

"Why, yes, I've been worried," the turnstone replied. "I've been afraid to leave my eggs, and I'm very hungry."

The fisherman, who knew all about hunger, said, "I'll be happy to watch your nest while you hunt for something to eat." So the turnstone flew off and gathered a tasty meal for herself. When she returned, the fisherman promised to return each day to watch her eggs while she hunted for more food.

For many days the fisherman caught many fish. And for many days he visited the turnstone. One day, after another good day of fishing, he walked onto the grassy shore to find the mother turnstone running after four baby turnstones.

"Oh, dear man, come see my beautiful babies," the turnstone exclaimed. The fisherman quietly approached the babies, who were beautiful indeed, and he even held one in his hand. Then the turnstone spoke softly to the fisherman.

"Tomorrow I will not be here. I must fly to another place to gather food for my babies. But next spring, and every spring after that, I will return to this lovely place. Since you were so kind to me, you will never be hungry. Even when others cannot catch fish, you will always catch all the fish you need." And with that, she led her family into the meadow.

The fisherman looked after her and smiled. Now he knew why he had caught so many fish. He sighed peacefully, content that his family would never be hungry again in the cold, long winters to come.

And to this day, turnstones nest in low, wet places near the grassy shores. They never go to the mountains anymore.

And if ever a fisherman sees a turnstone fly by, he knows he is likely to catch many fish. For the turnstone is a sign of good luck.

Discussion Questions:

1. During which part of the year do turnstones fly north?

2. At first, where did turnstones make their nests?

3. What did the mother turnstone leave in the fisherman's cap?

4. When the fisherman came ashore, where did he place the turnstone's egg?

5. When the fisherman went fishing from then on, what happened?

6. Why did the turnstones leave their new nesting place?

7. Where do turnstones now nest in the spring?

WHY THE TURNSTONES NEST NEAR THE SHORE
Puzzle

Name_____

Cut out the puzzle pieces below along the dotted lines.
On another piece of paper, arrange them in the correct order to make a picture.
Paste the puzzle pieces in place.
Color the picture.

MAPLE POPCORN TREATS

Canadian Indians heated corn in earthen jars over a fire until the kernels burst into white puffs. They then poured maple syrup over them to create popcorn treats.

Ingredients: 3 tablespoons vegetable oil
1 cup popcorn kernels
2 to 3 tablespoons maple syrup

How to Make:

1. Place oil in 4-quart electric frying pan and heat for 30 seconds.

2. Stir in kernels with wooden spoon and spread in one layer on bottom of pan.

3. Cover pan, leaving small opening for steam. When kernels begin to pop, shake pan gently until popping stops.

4. Remove popcorn and place in large bowl. Pour maple syrup on top and mix.

5. Wait one minute and serve. Gooey, but delicious! Makes 16 small servings.

CANADIAN INDIAN BREAD

Ingredients: 3½ cups water
1⅓ cups corn flour
1 teaspoon salt
1 cup blueberries or raisins
2–4 tablespoons butter
maple syrup to taste

How to Make:

1. Boil the water.

2. In a large bowl, mix corn flour and salt.

3. Pour boiling water onto the flour mixture, stirring constantly until it is thick.

4. Stir in blueberries or raisins.

5. Form the dough into two long bread rolls and chill until firm.

6. Use a knife to slice the dough into pieces. Fry in butter.

7. Serve with maple syrup. Makes 16 slices.

Name_____

Inuits hunted seals, polar bears, caribou, whales, and walruses. These animals
helped the Inuits stay alive in their cold land. Every part of an animal was used
for something—food, clothing, tools, and other things.

Look at the maze below.
Help the Inuit capture all the animals before going home to his igloo.
Trace a path through the maze.
Circle each animal you pass on your way to the igloo.

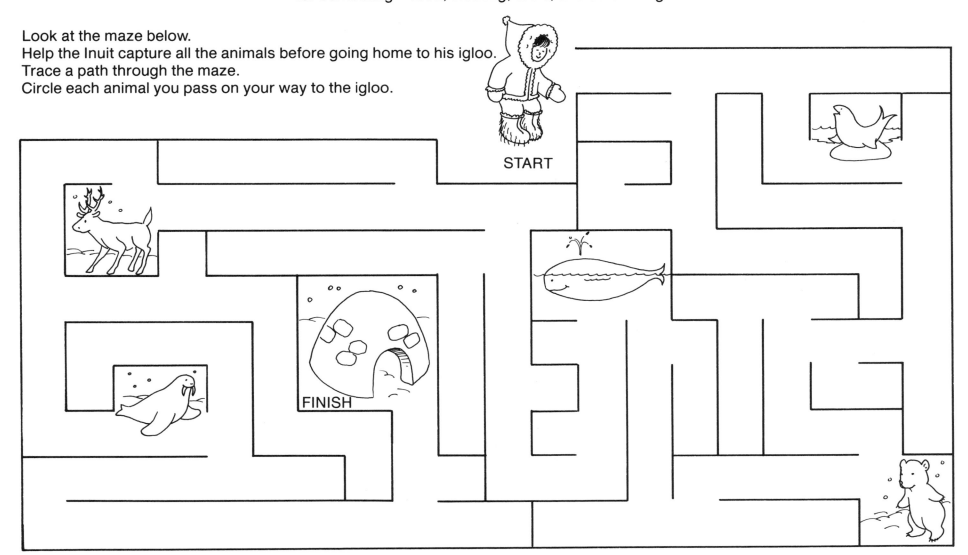

START

FINISH

O CANADA
Worksheet

Name_____

Add or subtract to solve each problem below.
Write the answer in each space.
Match your answers to the numbers in the Color Key.
Then color the spaces to show a symbol of Canada.

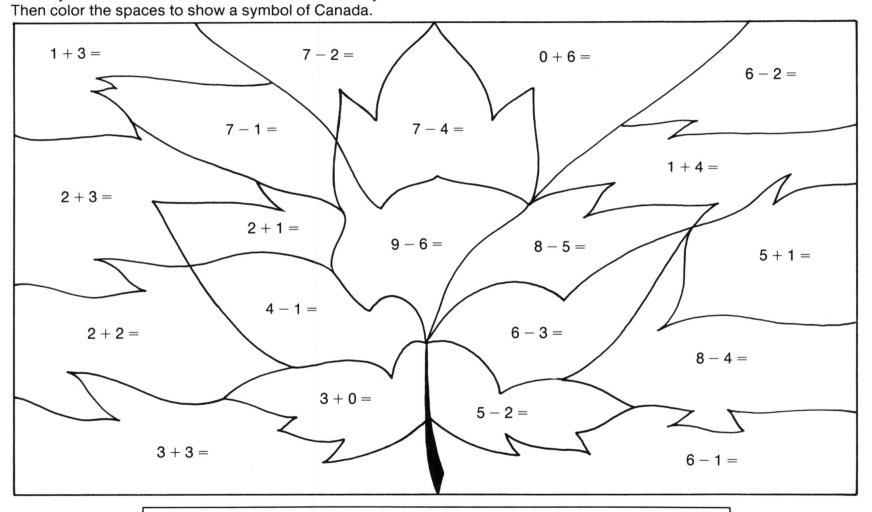

$1 + 3 =$

$7 - 2 =$

$0 + 6 =$

$6 - 2 =$

$7 - 1 =$

$7 - 4 =$

$1 + 4 =$

$2 + 3 =$

$2 + 1 =$

$9 - 6 =$

$8 - 5 =$

$5 + 1 =$

$4 - 1 =$

$2 + 2 =$

$6 - 3 =$

$8 - 4 =$

$3 + 0 =$

$5 - 2 =$

$3 + 3 =$

$6 - 1 =$

| **Color Key:** | 3=red | 4=brown | 5=yellow | 6=green |

Read the story on this page and page 20 to your class.
Then ask children the discussion questions that follow.

Long ago there lived an Indian boy named Tsem. Tsem was very small, but he was also very smart and brave. The other boys wouldn't let Tsem play with them because he was so small. So Tsem played by himself, wishing that someday the other boys would let him join in their games.

One day the others went into the forest to play. Tsem secretly followed them. He dodged quickly from tree to tree, trying to stay as close as possible to the others without being seen. Suddenly he saw something big and terrifying.

"Look out!" called Tsem. "The evil giantess Tsonerhwaw is hiding behind that cedar tree close to you!" The boys turned around and were angry to see little Tsem.

"You're lying," shouted the biggest boy. "You want to trick us because we won't play with you. Now go away."

"I speak the truth," answered Tsem. "Beware!"

Just then the ugly giantess sprang forward from behind the tree and grabbed Tsem. She dropped him into a huge basket she had woven from cedar roots. Tsonerhwaw stared fiercely into the eyes of the other boys, making it impossible for them to move. One by one, the giantess dropped the frightened boys into her basket. Then she closed the lid tightly and hung the basket over her shoulder as she walked slowly toward her home deep in the forest.

Inside the basket, all the boys except Tsem huddled together, crying and trembling. Only Tsem remained calm, trying to think of a way to escape. Then Tsem remembered the small knife he always carried with him. He took it from his belt and began to cut through the bottom of the woven basket. Soon he had made a small

hole. Tsem worked quickly, because he knew that as soon as the giantess reached her home, she would gobble up all the boys. In a moment the hole was just large enough for each boy to slip through.

Tsem whispered to the biggest boy, "You drop through the hole first, and then help catch the other boys as they jump from the basket." The boy put his legs through the hole, but then held on to the basket tightly, too afraid to let go.

"Jump now," urged Tsem. "There's not much time left." After a moment, the boy let go and fell to the ground. Then Tsem helped the other boys through the hole to safety. When they reached the ground, they began to run.

Tsonerhwaw had been so busy pushing through the thick bushes that she hadn't heard the boys escaping. But she stopped when the last boy accidentally kicked her leg with both feet as he swung from the basket.

Only Tsem was left in the basket. As he dropped through the hole, the giantess put her hand under the basket and caught him. The other boys looked back as they ran and saw that Tsem was trapped. They rushed back to their village to tell of Tsem's bravery and cleverness. When the chief heard their story, he said sadly, "Little Tsem had a bigger and braver heart than any of you."

The boys knew that Tsem had saved their lives. "If only Tsem would return," they wished. "Then we would never play a game without him."

Meanwhile, Tsem was in great danger. Tsonerhwaw lifted him up in her hand and glared as she opened her huge mouth to swallow him. Suddenly Tsem remembered a story about how a wise medicine man had once escaped from Tsonerhwaw. He held one finger in front of the giantess's eyes, making small circles in the air. Tsonerhwaw brought Tsem closer and closer to her mouth, but as she watched Tsem's finger moving in circles, her eyes began to blink. In an instant the ugly giantess was sound asleep. She fell to the ground with a loud thud, and Tsem climbed out of her hand and ran back to his home.

Everyone in the village was surprised and happy when Tsem returned. All the boys gathered round him and thanked him for saving their lives. And from that day on, Tsem's name was the first to be called whenever the boys played any games.

Discussion Questions:

1. Why didn't the children want to play with Tsem at first?
2. Why did Tsem follow the children to the forest?
3. What did Tsem try to warn the children about in the forest?
4. How did Tsem help the children escape?
5. Why did Tsem jump out last from the basket?
6. At the end of the story, why did the children like to play with Tsem?
7. Is size important when choosing friends? What is important?

SUPER SAND PAINTING
Craft Activity / Cutout

You need: cutouts on this page and page 22
scissors
sand
four cereal bowls
four different colors of food coloring or
powdered tempera paints
eight teaspoons
newspaper
four containers of glue
9″ × 12″ black construction paper

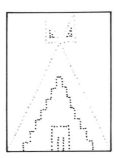

Steps:

1. Reproduce the cutouts on this page and page 22 several times. Cut them out along the dotted lines and have each child choose one.

2. Place equal amounts of sand into each bowl and add three or four drops of a different food coloring or a small amount of powdered tempera paint. Mix the coloring throughout the sand with a spoon.

3. Create four work areas and cover each with newspaper. Place a bowl of colored sand, two spoons, and a container of glue at each work area.

4. Divide the class into four groups, one to work at each area.

5. Children first decide which colors of sand to use on the various lines of their cutouts. Each child then applies glue to any lines he or she will cover with the sand at that work area. Each child sprinkles some colored sand onto the glued area. Excess sand is gently shaken onto the newspaper and then back into the bowl.

6. After a few minutes, move each bowl of colored sand to a different area and have children repeat step 5. Rotate the bowls from area to area until each group has had a chance to use each color of sand.

7. Children can then mount their pictures on the construction paper, using glue.

Variation:

Older children can design their own Indian sand paintings.

eagle

tepee

rain clouds

American Indians enjoyed all kinds of games and races that were not only fun but helpful in developing important skills: quickness of hands, feet, and eyes.

 RING BALL

You need: chalk
two different-sized balls (tennis ball and volleyball size)

Steps:

1. Draw a 12″ chalk circle on the playground surface.

2. Draw a chalk line, about 6′ away. Each child will stand behind it when throwing the ball. Adjust the distance according to age and ability of the children.

3. Place the smaller ball inside the circle. Each child in turn is given the larger ball. He or she must try to hit the smaller ball and knock it out of the circle while standing behind the chalk line.

4. Each time the smaller ball is knocked out of the circle, the child earns a point and takes another turn. That child continues until he or she misses the ball.

5. Each child plays three rounds. The winner is the player with the most points.

Variation:

Teams may be chosen. The first team to reach 20 points wins. Children may also be given more turns, depending on their interest.

ARROWHEAD RING TOSS

You need: masking tape
paper plate
three 5-oz. drinking cups
three embroidery hoops, about 10″ in diameter

Steps:

1. Tape the paper plate to the floor.

2. Place one of the drinking cups upside down and 6′ away from the paper plate. Tape it securely to the floor.

3. Turn each of the other two cups upside down and place them on either side of the first cup, at a distance of 5½′ from the paper plate and 3′ from the center paper cup. Tape the cups in place. This configuration should look like an arrowhead shape. See illustration.

4. Each player in turn stands on the paper plate and tries to toss a ring over a cup. The object is to get a ring around each cup. Each player tosses the three rings to see how many cups he or she can encircle. You can adjust the distance from cups according to the age and ability of children.

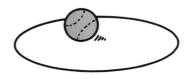

KICK STICK RACE

You need: chalk
several straight sticks

Steps:

1. On the playground, use chalk to mark off a starting point and a finishing point 25′ away.

2. Two to four players line up at the starting point for each race.

3. Each player then places a stick directly in front of his or her feet.

4. At the "Go" signal, the players kick the sticks along the surface of the playground to the finishing point using only their feet. A player who kicks his or her stick up into the air is eliminated from the race.

5. Then select additional groups of two to four children to compete in other races until each child in the class has had a turn.

6. Have the winners of each race compete in a final kick stick race.

Variation:

Play kick stick in teams. Each group of two children is given one stick. The children must kick it to one another, until they reach the finishing line. The first team to cross the line is the winner.

STOP-AND-GO RELAY RACE

You need: five empty 1-lb. coffee cans

Steps:

1. Place a coffee can upside down at a starting line and at every 10 yards for 40 yards.

2. Divide your class into two teams. One child from each team races at the same time. The first child on each team runs the whole distance and back, but must come to a full stop at each coffee can. When he or she returns to the starting line, the next child in line begins. All the children on the team take turns. The winning team is the one that finishes first.

WONDERFUL WEAVING
Art Activity

Weaving was an important and useful skill for many American Indian tribes. They used straw to weave baskets and wool or mountain-goat hair to weave blankets.

You need: 6″ paper plates (one for each child)
scissors
ruler
yarn
pictures of flowers from seed catalogs
  or magazines
glue

Steps:

1. Around the rim of each plate, cut seven evenly spaced slits toward the center, each about 1½″ long.

2. Measure and cut a 3′ piece of yarn for each child. Tie yarn around one of the seven sections of each paper plate. Knot the yarn at the back of the plate. Give one plate, with yarn attached, to each child.

3. Children will weave the yarn by bringing it forward through one slit and back through the slit next to it, around the rim of the plate.

4. Children continue weaving until all the slit sections of the plate are covered with yarn. If more yarn is needed to complete the weaving, tie a new piece of yarn to the end of the first piece. Remind children to keep pushing the yarn as close to the center of their plates as possible.

5. When all the sections of the plate are covered with yarn, knot the yarn in the back and cut off the excess.

6. Bring in photographs or pictures of flowers and ask children to do the same. Then have each child glue a picture onto the center of the plate.

Variations:

1. Arrange dried flowers in the center of each plate. Glue in place. Cover the flowers with clear plastic adhesive. Children may also glue small photographs of themselves onto the centers of their plates.

2. If bowl-shaped plates are used, children can use them as containers for clips, fasteners, or small toys.

You need: bowl
elbow macaroni
five different colors of tempera paints
five small paintbrushes
newspaper
3″ × 12″ pieces of felt (one for each child)
scissors
glue

Optional: shellac

Steps:

1. Fill the bowl with macaroni and set it, the paints, and the brushes on a table covered with newspaper.

2. Have several children at a time go to the art activity table. Each child takes one handful of macaroni and paints the individual pieces any colors he or she likes. Let the macaroni dry on the newspaper. If desired, spray or brush with shellac.

3. Give each child a 3″ × 12″ piece of felt. Have him or her cut the short ends of each strip into a **V** (see illustration), to make it easier to tie when finished.

4. Fringe one side of the felt along its length. Make fringes about 2″ deep. (Older children may be able to do this by themselves.)

5. Have children glue the colored macaroni on the unfringed part of the felt. They must leave room on both short ends so they can tie the bracelets around their arms or ankles. Let the glue dry.

Variation:

Children can sew macaroni (or beads) onto the felt. Show children how to bring the needle from the back through the felt, pulling the yarn through the tube of macaroni, and then poking the needle down through the felt again. After the pieces are sewn onto the felt, the child must tie a knot.

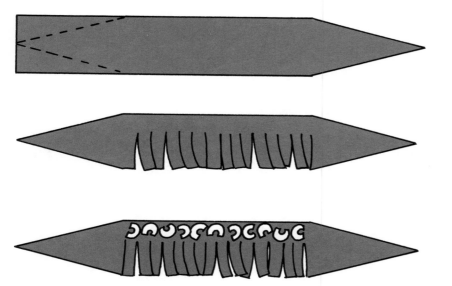

FIDDLE-DEE-DEE
Colonial Nursery Song

CHORUS
Fid - dle - dee - dee, Fid - dle - dee - dee, The fly has mar - ried the bum - ble - bee. 1. Said the fly, said he, "Will you mar - ry me, and live with me, sweet bum - ble - bee?" Fid - dle - dee - dee, Fid - dle - dee - dee, The fly has mar - ried the bum - ble - bee.

You need: bells and rhythm sticks

Steps:

1. Have children sit in a circle. Teach them the chorus to this song. Then have them clap out the beat as they sing.

2. Next, teach them the four verses, one at a time. Explain that the chorus is sung after each verse.

3. Assign individual children to play bells and rhythm sticks, for a count of four beats, after the word *ring* in the fourth verse. Children should continue the song after the four-beat pause.

Variation:

If desired, you can divide the class into boys, who will sing the fly's verse, and girls, who will sing the bee's verse. The remaining two verses can be sung by alternating boys with girls or by having the class sing together as a group.

Chorus
Fiddle-dee-dee,
Fiddle-dee-dee,
The fly has married the bumblebee.

Verse 2
Said the bee, said she, "I'll be 'neath your wing.
You'll never know I carry a sting."

Verse 3
So when Parson Beetle joined the pair,
They both went out to take the air.

Verse 4
Oh, the flies did buzz, and the bells did ring. (Pause.)
Did you ever hear so merry a thing?

OLD DAN TUCKER
Rhyming Song

Steps:

1. Have children sit in a circle. Sing the entire song to them. Then explain that Dan Tucker supposedly lived in the West many years ago. He did many silly things. Ask children to describe some of those things mentioned in the song.

2. Teach children the song, one line at a time.

3. When children know the entire song, add the actions suggested on this page.

Variation:

Have children make up new verses. Sing the first line of the verse and ask children to provide the second line ending with a rhyming word for *man*. Then sing the third line, asking for a fourth line ending with a rhyming word for *wheel*.

Verse

Old Dan Tucker was a fine old man, (Place hands on hips.)
He washed his face in a frying pan, (Rub hands over face.)
He combed his hair with a wagon wheel, (Move hand along hair.)
And ran with a toothache in his heel. (Hold heel in one hand and hop in place.)

Chorus

Clear the way for Old Dan Tucker! (Wave hand in shooing motion.)

He's too late to stay for supper. (Rub stomach.)
Supper's over, breakfast's cooking, (Rub stomach.)
Old Dan Tucker just stands there looking. (Place hand above eyes and look around.)

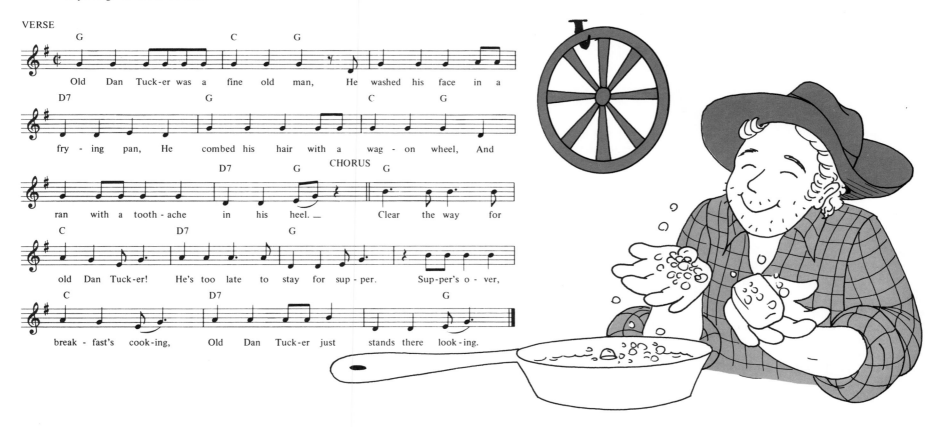

VERSE

Old Dan Tuck-er was a fine old man, He washed his face in a fry-ing pan, He combed his hair with a wag-on wheel, And ran with a tooth-ache in his heel. — Clear the way for old Dan Tuck-er! He's too late to stay for sup-per. Sup-per's o-ver, break-fast's cook-ing, Old Dan Tuck-er just stands there look-ing.

THE PILGRIMS
Story

Read the story to your class. Then reproduce the worksheet on page 30 for children to complete.

Long ago in England, the king would not let the Pilgrims pray in their own church. "You must go to my church," he demanded. The Pilgrims were very unhappy. They decided they would leave their homes.

At first the Pilgrims went to Holland. There they were free to pray in their own church, but they were still unhappy. They worked very hard in the cities, and yet they still were quite poor. They were also worried that their children would forget their English ways.

The Pilgrims decided to go to America, where they could have their own land, go to their own church, and bring their children up as English children. So 102 Pilgrims and many sailors sailed for America on a small sailing ship called the *Mayflower*.

For 66 days they sailed on the ocean. Their trip was long and hard. Many people became sick, and there wasn't enough food for everyone. Finally they saw land. A group of 16 men went to find a place to settle. They chose a spot that is now Plymouth, Massachusetts. There was a brook of fresh running water there and high ground where crops could be planted.

When the Pilgrims arrived, it was winter and very cold. Everyone worked hard. The men cut down trees and built houses. The women made clothes and prepared the food. But the winter was colder than it was in England. There was not enough to eat. Many people became sick and died. Only half the Pilgrims who sailed to America on the *Mayflower* lived through that first hard winter.

Finally, one spring day, Indians greeted the Pilgrims. Their chief, whose name was Massasoit, decided that the Indians and the Pilgrims could be friends. He said he would help the Pilgrims.

He sent Squanto, an Indian from his tribe who spoke English, to live with the Pilgrims. Squanto showed them where to fish and how to plant corn. He taught them to place dead fish in the soil along with the seeds to make the seeds grow better. He even showed them how to make flour and bread from corn.

When autumn came, the Pilgrims had plenty of food. They decided to set aside a day to thank God. They prepared a huge feast and invited their Indian friends. The feast lasted for three days. They ate, danced, sang songs, and played games. Everyone had such a good time that the Pilgrims decided to celebrate Thanksgiving every year.

Name_____

Look at the pictures below.
In the circle in each box, write a number from 1 to 4 to show the order of the pictures.
Cut apart the pictures along the dotted lines and put them in the correct order.
Color the pictures and then staple them together to make a minibook.

In the spring, the Indians taught the Pilgrims how to plant corn.

When autumn came, there was plenty of food. The Pilgrims made a feast and invited their Indian friends to the first Thanksgiving.

The king of England would not let the Pilgrims go to their own church.

The Pilgrims sailed to America on a ship called the *Mayflower*. Their trip was long and hard.

You need: light marker
ruler
8″ × 10½″ pieces of burlap
large yarn needles
different colors of yarn
scissors

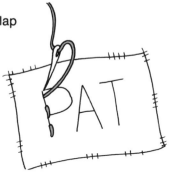

Steps:

1. With a light marker, carefully write each child's name, as well as your own, in 4″-high capital letters on individual pieces of burlap. Give each child a piece of burlap with his or her name on it, and keep your own piece.

2. Working with groups of two to three children at a time, thread a needle for each child with a 16″ length of any color yarn and make a knot at one end.

3. Show children how to pull the needle through the burlap without letting the yarn slip out of the needle's eye. Demonstrate how to sew stitches on your piece of burlap. Start at the beginning of the first letter, and bring the needle up through the back of the cloth to the front. Then insert the needle through the front of the cloth, about ½″ along the letter, to the back. Gently pull the yarn all the way through.

4. Repeat until you have completed half of the letter. Then let the children try sewing. Assist them if necessary. When the letter is completed, help each child knot the yarn and cut off the excess.

5. Have the children begin each new letter with a different-colored yarn. With younger classes, plan this activity to span several days. Each day, children can sew one or two letters of their names.

Variation:

Have children draw simple motifs (hearts, flowers, stars) with light marker on their pieces of burlap, and then stitch along the outlines. Mount each completed sampler by stapling it onto an 8½″ × 11″ piece of oaktag.

CANDLES FOR KIDS
Craft Activity

Explain that the early settlers made candles by twisting strips of cloth or string into wicks, and dipping them over and over into hot animal fat. They were then hung to cool and harden. Some settlers poured fat into molds that contained wicks. Have children make their own candles by using paraffin and milk containers for molds.

You need: clean, empty, half-pint milk containers (one for each child)
scissors
6″ lengths of string (one for each child)
pencils
double boiler
hot plate
4 lbs. of paraffin (found in a supermarket or a hardware store)
old crayons

Optional: candle scent (available at hobby or craft stores)

Steps:

1. Cut tops off the milk containers and give one container to each child, along with a pencil and a piece of string. Have each child tie one end of the string around the center of the pencil. Then ask each child to place the pencil across the top of the milk container so that the string hangs down into the center of the container almost to the bottom. (If the string is too long, have the child wrap it around the pencil once more.)

2. Fill the bottom of the double boiler with 3″ of water and bring to a boil over a hot plate. Put chunks of paraffin in the top of the double boiler and place it over the boiling water. Immediately reduce heat to simmer.

3. When the wax melts, add some old crayons to give the candles color. When the crayons melt, stir well.

4. Remove the double boiler from the hot plate. Let the wax cool for a few minutes. (If you wish, add scent just before pouring the wax.) Then pour the melted paraffin into each milk container until about 1″ from the top.

5. Let wax cool completely. This will take a few hours. When the wax is hard, cut each string just below where it is tied around the pencil, to make the wick. Children can peel the milk containers off and bring the candles home as gifts. (Makes about 14 candles.)

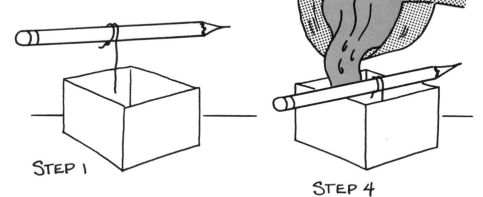

STEP 1

STEP 4

STEP 5

LET'S MAKE A HORNBOOK
Art Activity / Writing Activity

The early settlers' children went to one-room schoolhouses, where they learned to read and write using hornbooks. A hornbook is made of wood and looks like a paddle. The letters of the alphabet, written on a piece of paper, are placed over the wood. It is covered with a thin sheet of cow's horn to keep it clean. Use the instructions on this page and the pattern and cutout on page 34 to make hornbooks with your class.

You need: hornbook pattern and alphabet
cutout on page 34
scissors
pencils
oaktag
9″ × 12″ thin cardboard
glue
clear plastic adhesive
crayons
dry cloths

Steps:

1. Make one copy of the hornbook pattern and reproduce the alphabet cutout on page 34 for each child.

2. Cut out the hornbook pattern and trace it onto oaktag several times. Cut it out again. Have each child trace the oaktag pattern onto thin cardboard and cut it out.

3. Have each child cut out the alphabet cutout along the dotted lines.

4. Each child should glue the alphabet cutout onto the wide part of the cardboard paddle.

5. Cover the alphabet with clear plastic adhesive.

6. Children can practice tracing their letters with crayons. When they are finished, they can wipe their hornbooks clean with dry cloths.

Variation:

Prepare a cutout of numbers from 1 through 20 or a shape cutout for the hornbook. Have each child follow steps 3 through 5 to complete the hornbook.

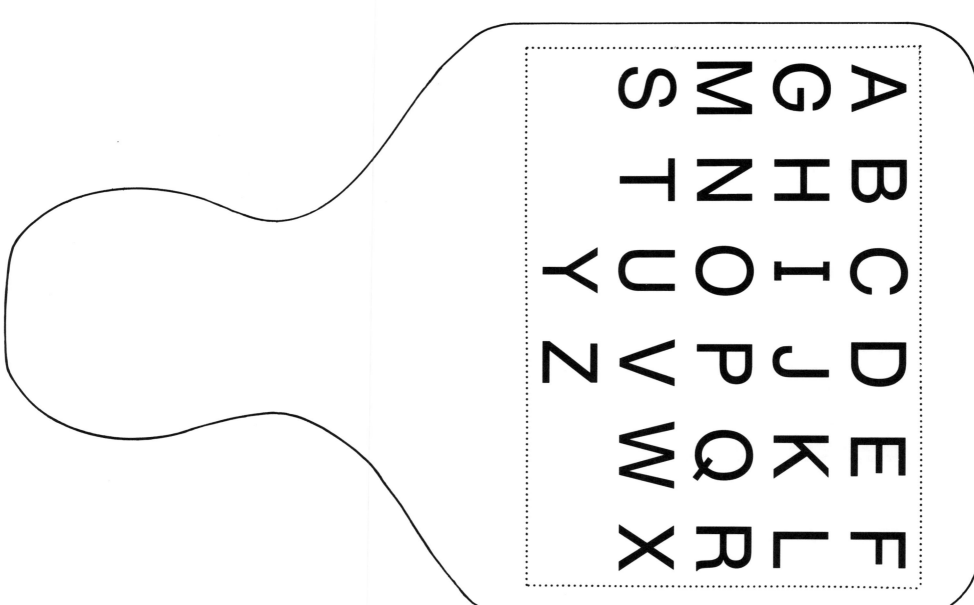

COLONIAL CRAFTS

Worksheet

Name ______________________

Find out what the four craftspeople shown below are making.
Cut out the pictures at the bottom of the page along the dotted lines.
Paste each picture in the box that shows the person who is making that object.

blacksmith

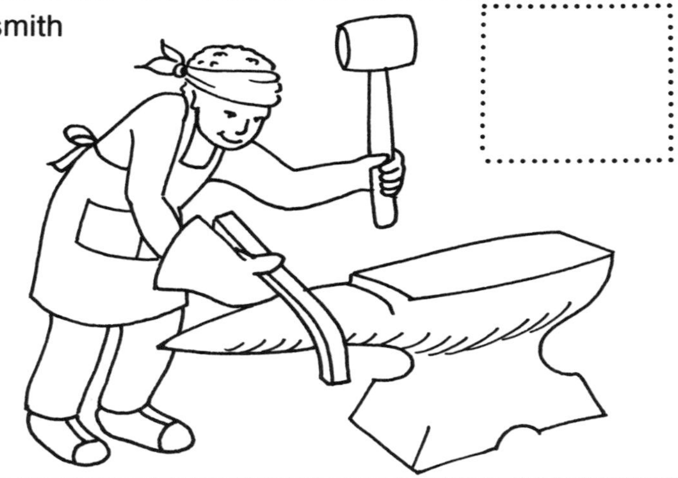

candlemaker

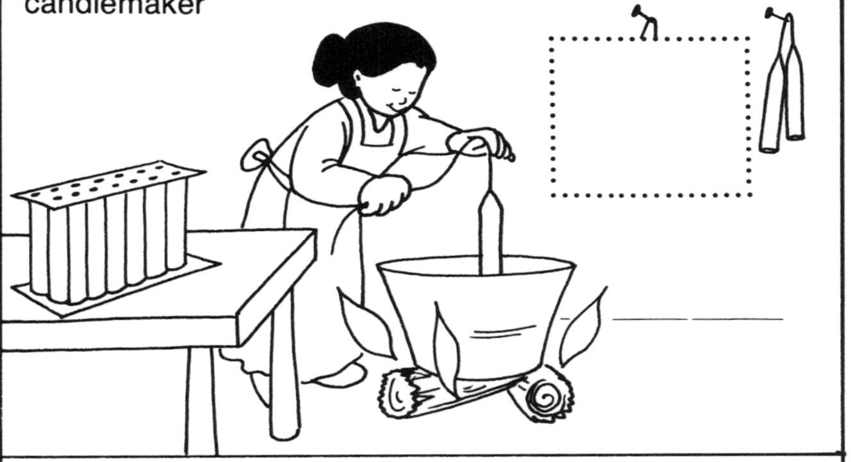

potter

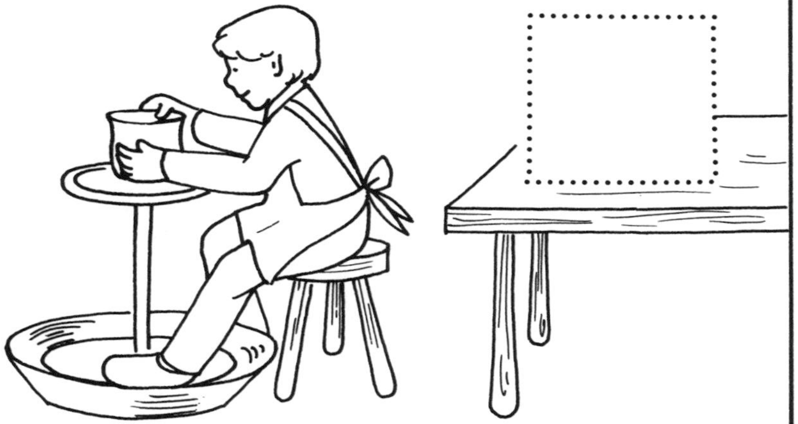

glassblower

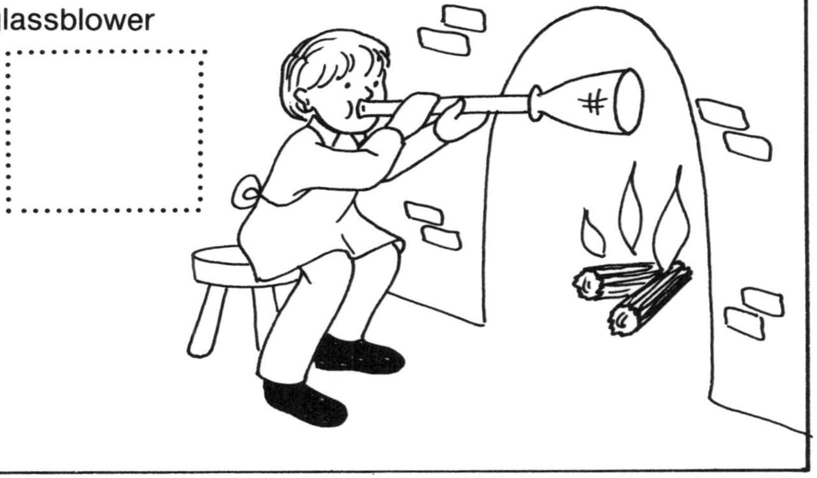

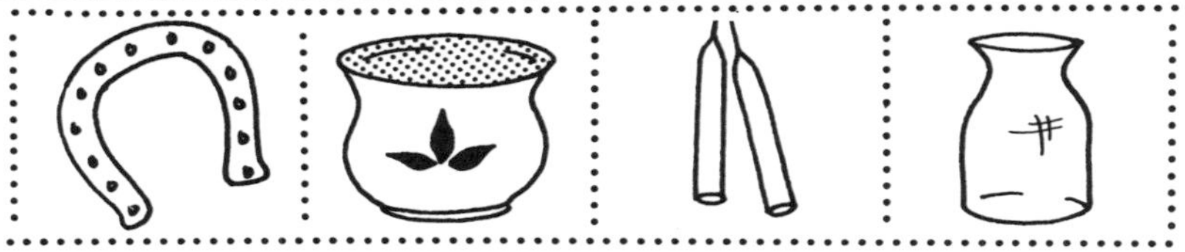

You need: ruler
scissors
thick red, white, and blue yarn
masking tape
string

Steps:

1. Measure and cut 12″ lengths of each color yarn for each child and for yourself.

2. Knot the three different-colored strands of yarn together at one end, making a set for each child and for yourself.

3. Have the children place the yarn on their desks, with the knot at the top, the blue yarn on the left side, white in the middle, and red on the right side. Ask children to tape the knotted ends to their desks, so the yarn does not slip while they are working.

4. Tape your yarn to the chalkboard for all to see. Demonstrate how to bring the blue yarn across the middle, over the white. Have children follow your example.

5. Next, tell children to bring their red pieces of yarn across their blue ones. Continue bringing alternate outside pieces over the middle, working from one side and then the other until about 1″ of yarn remains.

6. Measure and cut a 3″ piece of string for each child. Knot the string around the end of each braid.

7. Children can use their braids as decorative borders around picture frames or as bracelets or hair ribbons.

Follow-up Activities:

1. Bring in small braided rugs, place mats, and braided baskets for children to see. Explain how the early settlers braided yarn, wool, straw, and corn husks to make these useful items.

2. Children can make braided wall hangings. Measure and cut 24″ lengths of each color yarn for each child. Have children follow steps 2 through 6. Each child then winds the braid into a coil, and glues it onto oaktag. Use a hole puncher to make two holes, at either side of the oaktag, about 1″ from the top. Loop a 20″ length of yarn through the holes and knot the ends to make a hanger.

TOOLED TINSMITH TREASURE
Craft Activity

The tinsmith in colonial America was a metal craftsperson who was almost as busy as the blacksmith. In the winter, he made bed warmers, which held hot coals that warmed the colonists' feet. He also made candle holders, teapots, coffeepots, and different types of boxes.

You need: small boxes with lids
(one for each child)
aluminum foil
newspaper
drawing paper
ballpoint pens

Steps:

1. Have children bring in small boxes with lids. Give each child a piece of aluminum foil large enough to cover the bottom of the box. Have each child cover the bottom and sides of the box with the foil, shiny side facing out, and tuck any excess foil into the center.

2. Place thick layers of newspaper on a table. Give each child a piece of foil large enough to fit around the top of the box. Have each child put the piece of foil, shiny side down, on top of the newspaper.

3. Have the children smooth the foil sheets with their thumbs and thumbnails. Then have each child lay two pieces of drawing paper on top of the foil. Children will etch designs, using ballpoint pens, onto the paper. Tell them to press hard, but to take care not to rip the bottom layer of foil. Have children fill only the centers of the foil sheets with their designs.

4. Discard the drawing paper. Have each child turn the foil over so that the raised design is facing up. Help children to carefully wrap the etched foil around the tops of their boxes.

Variation:

For an antique look, mix a few drops of liquid detergent with black tempera paint. Lightly paint the etched foil. When it dries, lightly rub the foil with a soft paper towel. Polish each box gently, being careful not to smooth out the raised design.

THE ASTRONAUT
Action Story

Have the children stand in a large circle as you read about Neil Armstrong's flight to the moon. Let children act out the story as you tell it. Then have the children complete the worksheet on page 40.

It's July 16, 1969. I'm just waking up. *[All stretch.]* This is a special day for me. I'm Neil Armstrong and today I'm going to begin an important space flight. I'm the commander of the *Apollo 11* spaceship. I've trained for many years to be an astronaut. Day after day, year after year, I have practiced doing things on the earth that I will have to do in space. On this trip, I hope to be the first person to set foot on the moon. Want to come? *[Ask for responses.]* Good. Let's have a big breakfast before the flight. I'm having orange juice, steak, scrambled eggs, toast, and coffee. Come and join me. Let's eat. *[Move one hand to and from mouth.]* Now we'd better get into our space suits. *[All put on imaginary space suits.]* Since there will be no air to breathe in space, we have to wear these special suits in order to stay alive. Now let's go! Where's my crew? I'm looking for my lunar module pilot. *[Choose one child and give him or her a pretend hat.]* And where is my command ship pilot? *[Choose one child and give him or her a pretend hat.]* Good, now our crew is ready.

Let's go to the launching pad at the space center in Florida. *[All walk in place. Then cup hands over your eyes and look up.]* Look at the size of our spaceship!

Come on, let's get in the elevator that will take us up into the command module of our spaceship. *[Step into imaginary elevator, and press the button. Have children squat in position and gradually stand up while you make appropriate rising-scale sound to signify ascent.]* We're going up.

Here we are at the command module, our home for the next four days, until we get to the moon. Let's go in.

My, this command module is no bigger than the inside of a car. What do you see in it? *[Ask for responses.]* I see a few windows, an instrument panel, a computer, a radio, TV cameras, food, and couchlike seats where we can sleep. It's small, but it's comfortable—with air-conditioning, a bathroom, and a kitchen all included! Below us is the service module that holds the fuel, water, and gases needed during our flight. Let's get in our seats and buckle our seat belts. *[Children squat down.]*

It's time for blast-off. Let's test the control panel. Perfect! Ten seconds and counting. Let's do the countdown together, slowly. Ready? *[All count backward from ten to zero and shout, "Blast off!"]* Look at the blinding orange flame. Look at the white smoke! Slowly, slowly our spaceship is rising. The ground is shaking. *[Shake.]* Lift off! *Apollo 11* is on its way to the moon.

Now we're getting closer to the moon. The moon's gravity is pulling us toward the moon. We've got to climb into the moon lander through this small tunnel. *[Pretend to climb.]* Now it is July 20, four days after we began our space flight. On the thirteenth orbit around the moon, our moon lander will leave the command ship and start down to the moon. Our moon lander is separating from the command ship. We're going down. *[Children squat.]* Look at that giant crater. Oh no! Something is wrong with the computer. We're heading right for that crater! We have only 30 or 40 seconds of fuel left. We've got to land. Phew! We've safely passed the crater. We're landing.

At last we're here. Let's get ready to walk outside on the moon's surface, and when I take my first step, I have something special to say. Let's put on our boots, helmets, and gloves, and put on our portable life-support systems. *[Pretend.]* On the moon there is no air, water, plants, or animals. We need our life-support systems to help us stay alive. Our radio equipment will help us to talk to the command module and to people on earth. Now, down the nine-step ladder to the moon. Let's count each step. *[All count from one to nine, taking steps as if going down a ladder while counting.]* Now I'll set foot on the moon!

That's one small step for a man,
one giant leap for mankind.

The words I just said were the first words ever spoken on the moon. Do you think they will be remembered? *[Ask for responses.]* Now let's collect moon rocks and explore a crater. Then we'll climb back into our moon lander, return to the command ship, and go home to Earth. What an exciting adventure this has been!

Connect the numbered dots, beginning at 0.
Then color the picture.

Name_____

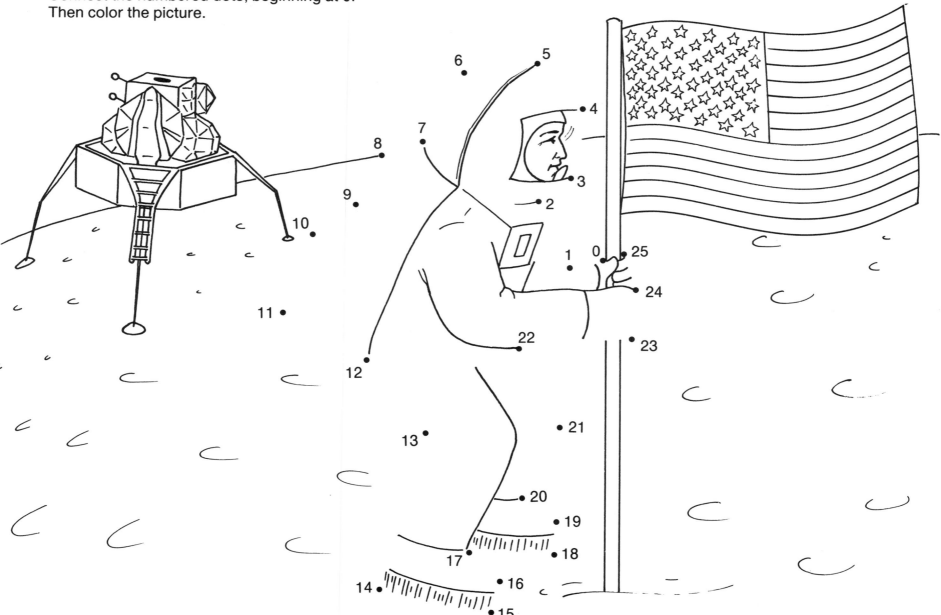

Read this story to your class. Then have children make Martin Luther King, Jr., booklets following the instructions on page 42.

Martin Luther King, Jr., a great black leader, grew up in a happy family in Atlanta, Georgia. When he was little, he liked to play football, baseball, and basketball. He always played to win, but he never liked to fight. If he saw boys or girls bothering someone, he would try to get them to stop.

Martin had many friends in his neighborhood, both black and white. But when he started school he noticed that the white children did not go to the same school as he did. He learned that there were certain places, like movie theaters and restaurants, where he and his family could not go because they were black. Martin knew this was unfair, but he didn't know how to change things.

Martin worked very hard in school. He liked to read all the time and often spent his allowance money on books. He did so well in school, he went to college when he was only 15 years old.

When he grew up, he became a minister like his father. He was a very good speaker, and people loved to hear him talk. His words could make people feel good inside, but they could also make them feel sad or angry. He made people want to do something about the unfair way that blacks were being treated.

Once Martin told people in his church that it wasn't fair that blacks had to sit in the backs of buses and give up their seats to white people if the bus was crowded. Martin wanted to change this law. He told blacks to stay off the buses until the law was changed. He said they should walk to work, take taxis, or ride with friends. He also told them that no matter what happened, they must not get into fights. Martin was convinced there was a better way of winning than by fighting with fists.

For a whole year, black people did not ride the buses, and the bus companies lost a lot of money. Finally, the law was changed so all people could ride and sit wherever they wished.

Martin Luther King worked hard all over the country to change unfair laws. He always told people to be honest, love each other, and work hard in order to hold up their heads and be proud of themselves.

In 1964, Martin won the Nobel Peace Prize for bringing love and peace to so many people. He received a medal and money, which he spent to help change laws so all people would be treated fairly.

In 1968, Martin Luther King was murdered by someone who didn't like Martin's ideas. The whole world was saddened to discover that a man who believed in love and peace had been killed.

Martin Luther King is no longer living, but his ideas will always be alive. He had a dream to make the world a better place for all men and women, and that dream still lives on. Each year, people throughout the United States celebrate Martin Luther King, Jr.'s birthday on January 15.

Discussion Questions:

1. Have you ever been treated unfairly? How did you feel?

2. Have you ever been sorry for treating someone badly? What did you do to make it up?

3. What did Martin Luther King, Jr., do to help people behave more fairly to each other?

4. What can children do to help people behave more fairly to one another?

You need: cutout on this page
scissors
12″ × 18″ different-colored construction paper
glue
8″ × 11″ lined writing paper
pencils

Steps:

1. Reproduce the cutout on this page, one for each child.

2. Have children cut them out.

3. Distribute the construction paper. Each child folds it in half to form a booklet and glues the cutout onto the cover.

4. Write the sentence starters below on the chalkboard.

5. Distribute the writing paper and pencils and have children copy and complete the sentence starters on it. Younger children can dictate their sentences.

6. Have children glue their sentences inside the booklets.

Sentence Starters

To get along better with my family, I can . . .
I can get along with my friends at school by . . .
If someone treats me unfairly, I can . . .
To help a friend who is unhappy, I would . . .

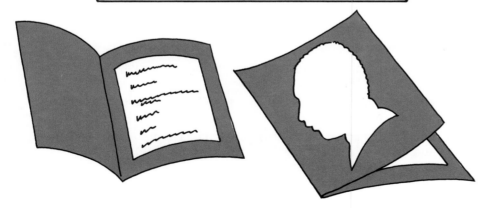

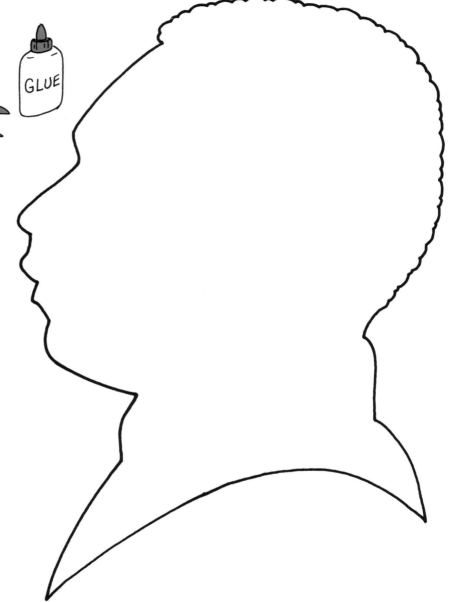

Read this story to your class. Then reproduce the worksheet on page 44 for children to complete.

Amelia Earhart was born in Kansas in 1898. Even when she was young, she always wanted to do something brave and exciting. But all the exciting things were being done by boys. When she grew up, she decided to serve the United States as a nurse during World War I. While she was doing this work, she watched airplane pilots learning how to fly. "That's what I want to do!" she thought. From then on, she worked hard to save her money to take flying lessons.

Amelia Earhart became an excellent pilot. She set many records for flying at high speeds. She was also the first woman to fly across the Atlantic Ocean. But on that trip she was only the airplane's log keeper, writing information about the flight. It bothered her that she had not flown the plane herself and worked its controls. Four years later, she planned another trip. This time she would fly across the ocean alone.

That flight was a very difficult one. Amelia brought only a thermos of hot soup and a can of tomato juice on the famous trip. Soon after the plane took off from Newfoundland, Canada, the clouds grew thick, and hard rain pounded the windshield. Lightning flashed around her plane and thunder boomed. Some of the plane's instruments broke down. Then ice formed on the wings, and the plane began to spin out of control. Luckily Amelia's many years of flying enabled her to regain control. Later on, fuel started to leak into the cockpit. The stinging fumes from the gasoline burned Amelia's eyes and nose.

Even though she was tired, stiff, and hungry, Amelia kept her eyes on the instruments and her hands on the throttle. At last she saw a thin, dark line ahead of her. It was land. Fifteen hours and 18 minutes after takeoff, Amelia landed on the other side of the ocean, in Ireland. At the age of 34, she was the first woman to pilot a plane alone across the Atlantic Ocean. Everyone was very proud of Amelia Earhart. She had accomplished her dream.

Discussion Questions:

1. What kind of work did Amelia do during World War I?

2. How did Amelia become interested in flying?

3. What did Amelia do that made her so famous?

4. What problems did Amelia face while on her famous trip?

Name_____

Help Amelia Earhart find her way across the ocean.
Trace a flight path for her.
Keep the plane away from bad weather.

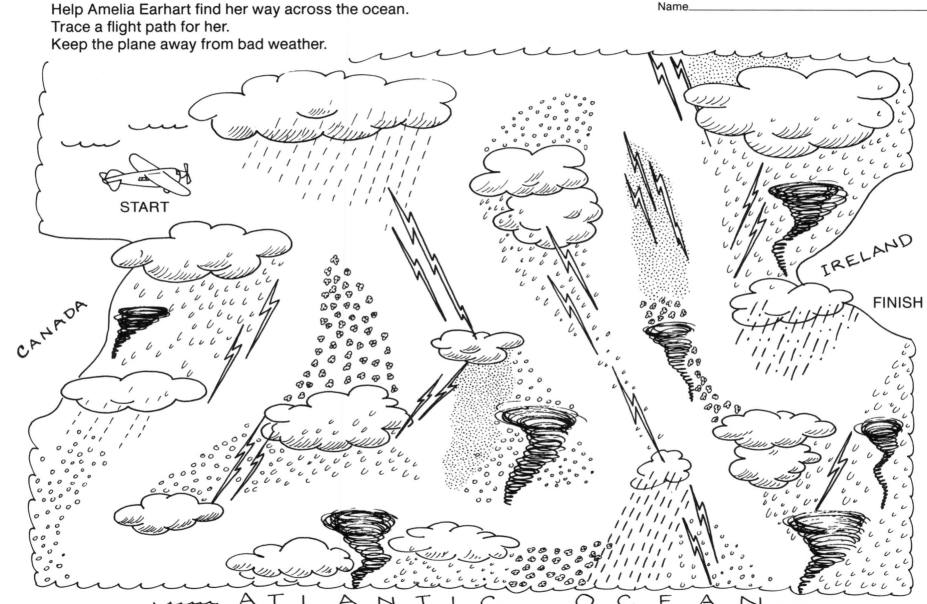

Read the story of George Washington to your class. Then reproduce the worksheet on page 46 for the children to complete.

George Washington was the first president of the United States. He was born in 1732 in Virginia, where his father owned a big tobacco farm. George's father was a rich man and gave George many fine things, including his own horse. George loved to ride around the country-side and through the woods near his family's farm. His friends often said he was the best rider in Virginia.

As a young man, George became a surveyor. A surveyor is a person who measures the land so people know where one farm ends and another begins. As he did this, he saw how beautiful and wonderful America was. He decided that one day he would like to help his country.

When he was older, George had his chance. He became a soldier in the Continental Army. Soon after, he was made a general, and when the War of Independence started, George was picked to be the commander in chief of all the soldiers in the army. George was very brave and smart, and he knew how to fight well. But he had a very hard job to do. Many of his soldiers had never been in an army before. Some soldiers were young boys, while others were storekeepers or frontiersmen. The soldiers didn't always have enough to eat or enough warm clothing to wear in the winter. After a while their boots wore out too, and only a few were able to get other pairs.

George led his men for many years, until the war was over. Afterward, the people of the new country, the United States, elected him to be their first president. We remember George Washington as a great hero who helped his country in war and in peace. The capital of the United States, Washington, D.C., is named after George Washington.

Discussion Questions:

1. Where was George Washington born?

2. What did he like to do as a boy?

3. What kind of work did George Washington do as a surveyor?

4. What kind of problems did George Washington's soldiers have during the War of Independence?

5. What job did George Washington have after the War of Independence?

GEORGE WASHINGTON
Make a Minibook

After you have heard the story of George Washington, look at the pictures and read the sentences below. In the circle in each box, write a number from 1 to 4 to show the order of the pictures. Then cut out the boxes along the dotted lines, and put them in the correct order. Color the pictures and staple them together to make a minibook.

Name _____

☆ ☆ ☆ ☆ ☆ ☆ ☆ ☆ ☆

After the War of Independence, George Washington was elected the first president of the United States.

George Washington became the commander in chief of the Continental Army during the War of Independence.

As a young boy, George Washington loved to ride horses.

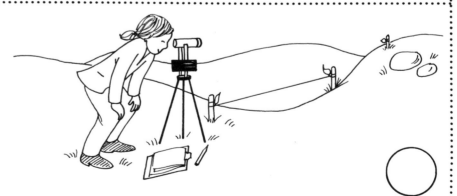

When George Washington was a young man, he became a surveyor.

Read the story of Abraham Lincoln to your class. Then reproduce the worksheet on page 48 for the children to complete.

Abraham Lincoln grew up in a log cabin deep in the woods of Kentucky. When he and his sister were little, they had so many chores to do at home, they didn't have much time left for school. But Abe loved to learn and always looked forward to going to school, although he had to walk many miles. There Abe learned to read, write, and do arithmetic. At home, Abe didn't always have a pencil or paper to use when he studied, so sometimes he would write with charcoal on the back of a shovel. But he didn't mind. It was so wonderful to learn.

When Abe grew older, he had many jobs. He was so big and strong, he would split logs, plow fields, cut corn, and thresh wheat. He also worked in a country store, where people would come to buy things and to listen to Abe's jokes and stories. One day a woman bought some apples and gave Abe too much money. That night, when Abe realized it, he walked many miles to give the extra money back to her. Soon everyone was calling him "Honest Abe."

Abe decided that he wanted to become a lawyer and help poor people. As he traveled from town to town, he was very sad to see that some people were slaves. These men and women had no freedom at all. Sometimes they were taken from their homes and sold from one owner to another. Children were even taken away from their mothers and fathers. Abe, who was a very good speaker, made speeches against slavery. He said that all people were born free. Many people in the United States listened to him and also felt slavery should be stopped. When Abe was elected the sixteenth president of the United States, many years later, he decided to do something about it.

Soon after he became president, a terrible war started in the United States. Many people in the Southern states wanted to keep slaves, and they fought people in the Northern states who wanted all people to be free. After a long war, the Northern states won. The slaves were freed, and Abraham Lincoln had made it possible.

Today a great monument, the Lincoln Memorial, stands in Washington, D.C., so we can always remember the great president who fought for the freedom of all people.

Discussion Questions:

1. Where did Abraham Lincoln grow up?

2. What kinds of jobs did Abe Lincoln have as a young man?

3. Why was Abe Lincoln called "Honest Abe"?

4. Why did Abe Lincoln think that slavery was wrong?

After you have heard the story of Abraham Lincoln, look at the pictures and read the sentences below. In the circle in each box, write a number from 1 to 4 to show the order of the pictures. Then cut out the boxes along the dotted lines, and put them in the correct order. Color the pictures and staple them together to make a minibook.

Name _____

A statue of Abraham Lincoln stands in Washington, D.C., so that we will always remember him.

When he became president, Abraham Lincoln made a law against slavery.

Abraham Lincoln became a lawyer when he was a young man.

Abraham Lincoln did his homework on the back of a shovel, using charcoal.

Read this story to your class. Then reproduce the worksheet on
page 50 for children to complete.

Long ago, the North Woods was a wild place full of tall trees. The rivers were faster then, the winters colder, the snows deeper, and the people bigger. And the biggest person of all was Paul Bunyan.

Paul was the biggest baby the world has ever seen! When he rolled over in his sleep, trees fell down for miles around. Men had to nail the broken trees together to make a cradle for him. When Paul was old enough to go to school, he was too big to fit inside the schoolhouse. And he couldn't even learn to read, because the letters were too small. Paul was very sad that he never learned to read and write. He soon headed west to become a logger. In four steps he was halfway there.

Paul was a powerful logger, the best who ever lived. People still talk about the way he would cut through the biggest trees as if they were butter. He could slice through ten trees at a time with one stroke of his ax. And all the trees would fall over in a straight line, too! But Paul had one problem. He was hungry all the time. At the loggers' camp, the cook had only one small pan and simply could not make pancakes fast enough for Paul.

"I'll fix that," said Paul. He went to his farmer friends and asked them for their old plows. Then he took off the front end of each shovel-shaped plow and hammered them all together. He used more plow shovels than you can count, and finally made a giant griddle out of them. It was so wide that the other loggers took turns skating across it with bacon on their shoes. When the bacon was cooked, the griddle was ready for pancakes. Now the cook could make all the pancakes he wanted on that one huge griddle.

It was always cold in Minnesota when Paul lived there, but the winter of the blue snow was the coldest winter of all. When people talked, their words froze in the air. It took till the spring thaw before you could understand what people had been saying. And the snow came down all in blue flakes. There were blue snowdrifts ten feet tall. One day Paul went looking for his lost dog in the blue snow. He walked as far as the North Pole in his snow shoes. The dog found his way home all by himself, but when Paul returned, he was carrying a great big blue baby ox. Paul named his blue ox Babe. Babe grew to be as big an ox as Paul was a man. Once a crow, perched on one of Babe's horns, set out to fly across to the other horn. It took that crow all winter to fly across!

Paul and Babe always worked together, pulling the curves and bumps out of logging roads, or standing at either end of a turning river and pulling until the river was straight. Paul and Babe became famous throughout the land for their amazing feats.

Paul Bunyan needs the biggest clothes and tools that can be found.
Look at the objects in the boxes below.
In each box, circle the biggest object or pair of objects.
Color the pictures you circled.

Name

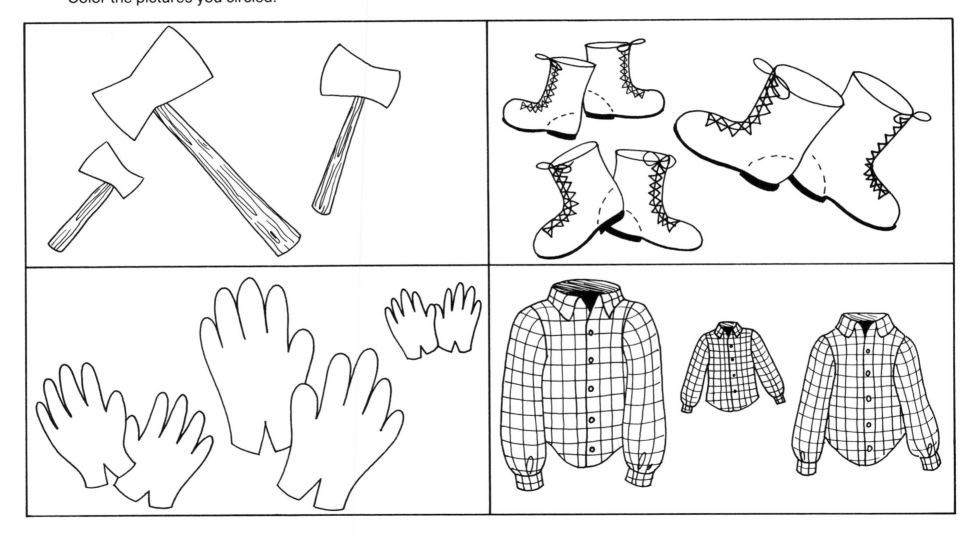

Read this story to your class. Then have children complete the craft activity on page 52.

Davy Crockett lived in the wilderness many years ago. He loved to hunt in the woods and fish in the streams, and everywhere he went he wore his coonskin cap. Davy knew all about the creatures of the forest. Some were very smart and others were not too bright. But the smartest creature Davy ever met was a big brown bear.

This particular bear used to follow Davy wherever he went. The bear became so tame, he would come into the house and warm up by the fireplace on cold days. One day Davy taught the bear to play checkers. Every evening Davy and the bear would sit in the living room playing the game together. Sometimes Davy won, but it was usually the bear who did.

"Just what are you thinking?" Davy would sometimes ask the bear. Then Davy would look into the bear's eyes and see how gentle and kind he was. The bear would never speak, but Davy knew that the bear understood everything he said.

One day Davy called the bear over. "Look here," he said. "I want you to earn your keep." Davy showed the bear how to fill the churn with milk and stir the milk until it turned to butter. Then he taught the bear to scramble eggs, grill bacon, mix the bear's favorite pancake batter, and bake cherry pies. After that, the bear did all the cooking.

The bear became so civilized he even set the table for meals. He ate dinner each night with Davy, and then he washed and dried the dishes. In fact, he never broke a plate.

One day, the bear decided to move to town and open up his own inn. He called it the Brown Bear Inn. He served his famous Bear Pancakes with homemade butter and lots of honey. People came from miles around to taste them. At first Davy was sad at losing a good friend, but soon the bear was such a success that Davy couldn't help but become happy again.

DAVY'S COONSKIN CAP
Craft Activity

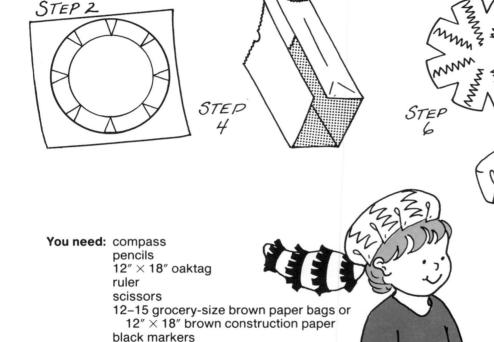

You need: compass
pencils
12″ × 18″ oaktag
ruler
scissors
12–15 grocery-size brown paper bags or
   12″ × 18″ brown construction paper
black markers
stapler
9″ × 12″ brown and black construction paper
glue

Steps:

1. Use a compass to draw a 12″ circle on oaktag. Then draw a 9½″ circle inside it.

2. Use a ruler to draw eight equidistant triangles between the 9½″ circle and the 12″ circle. (See illustration.)

3. Cut out the 12″ circle and the triangles inside it. Trace it several times onto oaktag and cut out these cap patterns.

4. Use scissors to cut down one side of each paper bag and cut off the bottom. Flatten the bags. Brown construction paper can be used instead of bags.

5. Have each child trace and cut out an oaktag cap pattern on a bag or on construction paper.

6. The children then use black markers to draw zigzag "raccoon stripes" on their paper caps, as shown.

7. Help each child overlap and staple the flaps between each triangular cut. This will form the cap's shape.

8. To form the tail of the cap, each child rolls a piece of 9″ × 12″ brown construction paper into a tube about 3″ in diameter. Staple one end together and flatten the tube.

9. Ask the children to use scissors to round off the unstapled ends of the tails.

10. Measure and cut the black construction paper into 1½″ × 9″ strips. Give each child four strips. Demonstrate how to create fringe by making 1″ cuts along one side of each strip.

11. The children then glue the strips around the tails of their caps, forming "raccoon" fur stripes, as shown.

12. Staple the straight ends of the tails to the backs of the caps.

Read the story below to your class. Sing the verses of the song to the tune of "Oh, Susannah," as they appear in the story. Then teach the children the song and have them sing it as it appears when you reread the story.

Mike Fink was as straight and thin as a bean pole and as rugged as an ox. His hair was bright red and it reached to his shoulders. His tanned face was covered with whiskers. He wore a coonskin cap tilted over one ear.

Mike was a strong, clever scout and boatman. When Mike bought his keelboat, the *Lightfoot,* he became the youngest keelboat captain ever. A keelboat was a long, narrow boat made to float in shallow water. Keelboats could carry a lot of weight and move very fast. To move his keelboat upstream, Mike had to use a pole to pull and push it, and a paddle to keep it going. If the boat wasn't going fast enough, the men would row the keelboat and sing together.

First the men would sit in the boat and skim the oars over the water. Then they would stand up and sink their oars deep into the river, pulling the boat along so hard that the oar handles would bend. Let's help the boatmen row and sing.

> *Oh, work harder, men, and faster too,*
> *Our keelboat moves too slow.*
> *We're on our way to Shawneetown,*
> *A long, long time ago.*
> *Hi-ho ho-ho, just watch our keelboat go,*
> *Rowing up the river on the O-hi-o-hi-o.*

Then the men would rest a few minutes. When the river narrowed and the current was too strong for oars, the men would have to "bushwhack." They would steer close to shore, grab hold of some bushes, and pull on the bushes to move the boat along the way.

Let's help the men move the keelboat up the river! Stand up and pull hand over hand as we sing.

> *Oh, work harder, men, and faster too,*
> *Our keelboat moves too slow.*
> *We're on our way to Shawneetown,*
> *A long, long time ago.*
> *Hi-ho ho-ho, just watch our keelboat go,*
> *Bushwhacking up the beautiful O-hi-o-hi-o.*

Another way to make the keelboats go upstream was by "poling." The men took long poles, and each person stood in a place along the narrow running boards on the sides of the boat. Mike Fink, the captain, would command, "Set poles." Each man would drop the iron-tipped end of his pole over the side of the boat and set it firmly in the mud on the bottom of the river. "Down the poles," Mike would command. At this, each man would place one end of his pole against a leather pad on his shoulder, bend low, and force his way from the front of the keelboat to the rear with the greatest effort. As the last man on each side would reach the rear, Mike would shout, "Lift poles." Then the men did just that, hurrying back to begin again. Beneath them the keelboat inched forward. Let's help them pole the keelboat as we sing along with the men.

*Oh, work harder, men, and faster too,
Our keelboat moves too slow.
We're on our way to Shawneetown,
A long, long time ago.
Hi-ho ho-ho, just watch our keelboat go,
Poling up the river on the O-hi-o-hi-o.*

Steering a keelboat against strong and powerful currents with rocks, logs, and other keelboats on every side discouraged many men. But to Mike Fink it was an adventure. The river was stubborn, full of surprises, and it demanded every ounce of his strength. But when Mike Fink was fighting the great Ohio River he was the happiest man alive.

Discussion Questions:

1. What kind of work did Mike Fink do?

2. What is a keelboat?

3. How did Mike Fink and his men move their keelboat up the river?

4. What did the men do when they "bushwhacked"?

5. What did the men do when they "poled" up the river?

6. Why was it difficult to be a keelboat man?

Read the story on this page and page 56 to your class. Then reproduce the maze on page 57 for children to complete.

Big Mose was the best fire fighter in old New York. He could put on his fire hat and fire coat faster than anyone else in town. With a single leap, he could jump straight into his boots, two yards away. He had to be careful when he put on his socks, though. He was so strong, he might poke his feet right through them. Big Mose polished the brass on his fire engine shinier than anyone else could. He made the brass so bright people could read their newspapers by the light it gave off! But, most important of all, Big Mose could put out fires faster than anyone else.

In those days, New York did not pay fire fighters for their dangerous work. Instead, every fire fighter was a volunteer. They rode in fire trucks pulled by strong horses. The fire trucks carried water pumps, hoses, and ladders over cobblestone streets to the fires. Once there, the fire fighters worked together to drag the heavy hoses as close to the fire as they could get. But Mose was so strong, he could pull the hose to a second floor all by himself. He was so fast, he could climb up one side of a ladder and down the other side while the ladder still balanced straight up in the air. And he was so big, he could often stamp out a fire all by himself, with his great big feet.

But one day there was a fire Mose could not stamp out alone. It was a huge fire in a four-story building near the Hudson River. Clouds of black smoke poured out of the windows and flames leaped high in the air. Mose and the other fire fighters drove their horses toward the fire, pulling the engines behind them.

Mose yelled, "Start pumping, friends! I'll climb to the roof and chop a hole in it. Then we can pour water down onto the fire from above." The roof was so high, Mose had to tie two of the tallest ladders together in order to reach it. He bravely made his way up the long, swaying ladder. But when he reached the roof, there was a great explosion. The building had been filled with fireworks! The flames had reached the fireworks just as Mose reached the roof, and hundreds of firecrackers started exploding all at once. The walls of the building shook, and the roof shot up, up, up into the air like a rocket. And who was standing on top of the roof? It was Big Mose, the fire fighter!

Then, suddenly, the roof started to fall. Never before had Big Mose been in such a fix. But Big Mose kept his head. He noticed that when he moved his body, the roof shifted in midair. By leaning this way and that, he found that he could guide the falling roof with the help of the wind under it. But then the wind began to die down and the roof began to fall again. Mose didn't want to crash. He was determined to make a landing he could be proud of. All the people of New York had their eyes on him and his flying roof.

Mose looked down. The fire was spreading rapidly. He glanced at the nearby Hudson River. Suddenly, Big Mose had an idea. "Maybe I can put out the fire and have a perfect landing, too," he thought.

He leaned back, and the roof began to glide toward the river. "I have to do this exactly right," he thought. "If I lean too far, the roof will flip over and I'll fall off." As the roof glided closer to the river, Mose leaned forward. The roof skimmed the river with a terrific force, making a tremendous wave. The roof bounced up and then hit the water again, making another huge splash. The two waves crashed and started rolling toward the shore. The crowd stopped cheering for Mose and instead ran for cover. In a moment, the waves hit the burning building. Splash! Splash! The fire was out.

Big Mose, the hero fire fighter, swam to shore. The crowd went wild, cheering for him and waving their hats in the air. The other fire fighters lifted their hero way up and put him on top of his fire engine. Bells clanged, whistles blew, and everyone chanted, "Big Mose, Big Mose!" Big Mose was the hero of all New York, the best and bravest fire fighter who ever lived.

Discussion Questions:

1. Where did Big Mose live?

2. What kind of work did Big Mose do?

3. Onto what did Big Mose climb to help put out the big fire near the Hudson River?

4. Where did Big Mose and the roof finally land?

5. What did the crowd of people do when Big Mose swam to the shore?

HELP FIGHT THE FIRE!
Maze Worksheet

Help Big Mose get to the fire as quickly as he can.
Start at the fire truck. Trace the path with your pencil.
Stay within the lines.

Name_____

JOHN HENRY AND THE STEAM DRILL
Tall Tale

Read the story on this page and page 59 to your class. Then reproduce the worksheet on page 60 for children to complete.

John Henry was a black man who lived in the South more than 100 years ago. He hammered steel rods deep into mountains and helped to build tunnels so that the railroad could go through. People say that John Henry was born with a hammer in his hand.

As a baby, John Henry liked to play with little pieces of steel and his father's five-pound hammer. He could break apart all the stones he could find. While some babies slept with bottles and others with blankets, John Henry slept with his hammer.

With all this hammering and pounding, it was only natural that John Henry grew up to be a big and powerful man. By the time he was 15 years old, he was bigger and more powerful than any man around. He picked cotton for a while; and he even worked on a steamboat. But he never felt really happy.

One day, John Henry heard the ring of hammers and the songs of other black men working in the distance. He followed that ringing and came to a big mountain. "That's the finest music I've ever heard," John Henry exclaimed. The men were at work, hammering and singing as they built the Big Bend Tunnel for the C & O Railroad. John Henry saw the men pounding steel rods deep into the rock of the mountain, and he knew then what he wanted to do.

As John Henry watched, his eyes lit up. "I'm a natural-born steel-driving man," he said. "I'm going to be the best steel-driver in the world." And sure enough, he was. John Henry soon could drive more steel than any nine men at work on the Big Bend Tunnel.

Everything was just fine until one day a smart-talking salesman with a strange, big machine came along. He was bragging to the captain of the crew that his new steam drill could drill a hole faster than 20 men using hammers. Besides that, it didn't have to rest or eat, so it could save the captain a lot of money. The captain seemed interested, but he was really very fond of his men, particularly John Henry. So he made a deal.

He said, "Tell you what. We'll have a race between the steam drill and the best steel-driving man I've got. If the steam drill wins, I'll buy it, but if John Henry wins, you give me the steam drill and $500." And that's how the great showdown began.

"Well!" John Henry exclaimed. "No steam drill's ever going to drive steel like a man. That takes muscles, not steam, and muscles I've got." So the contest was on, man against machine.

John Henry swung the hammer with his usual powerful and steady rhythm. The hammer rose and fell, rose and fell, rose and fell. And John Henry began to sing to mark the time.

As he worked, John Henry looked over at the steam drill. He saw that the machine was drilling faster than he was. So John Henry put down his nine-pound hammer and picked up two 20-pound hammers. He kept on pounding, a hammer in each hand. He worked so hard that the handles of the hammers grew too hot to hold. So he put them down and grabbed two more.

Meanwhile the steam drill's engine smoked, sparked, and glowed with fire. The gears clashed violently. It gobbled tons of coal and barrels of water.

Hour after hour the contest went on. The smooth and even rhythm of John Henry's 20-pound hammers rang out above the noise of the machine. But above it all, John Henry's voice could be heard, for when there was a hammer in his hand, there was a song on his lips.

All day and into the night the contest continued. Just when John Henry wondered how long his muscles would last, the machine made a terrible noise. The valves blew out, the boiler split open, the machine sputtered and choked, and then it broke down. There was a sudden silence in the tunnel, except for the ring, ring, ring of John Henry's hammers. John Henry had won! But he didn't stop. He pounded those hammers a dozen more times until he broke right through the mountain! The Big Bend Tunnel was finished.

John Henry turned around, looked back down the long, black tunnel, and then slid down against a rock. He pulled his hammer close to his heart and said, "I've done all I'm supposed to do. I drove more steel than the steam drill and now I'm done." John Henry closed his eyes and never got up again.

The preacher came and read the burial services at the tunnel. And there they buried John Henry, with a hammer in his hand.

HAMMER HUNT
Worksheet

Name____________________________________

Help John Henry build the railroad.
Look at the picture below to find John Henry's hammers.
Circle them. Then color in the picture.

How many hammers did you find?_________

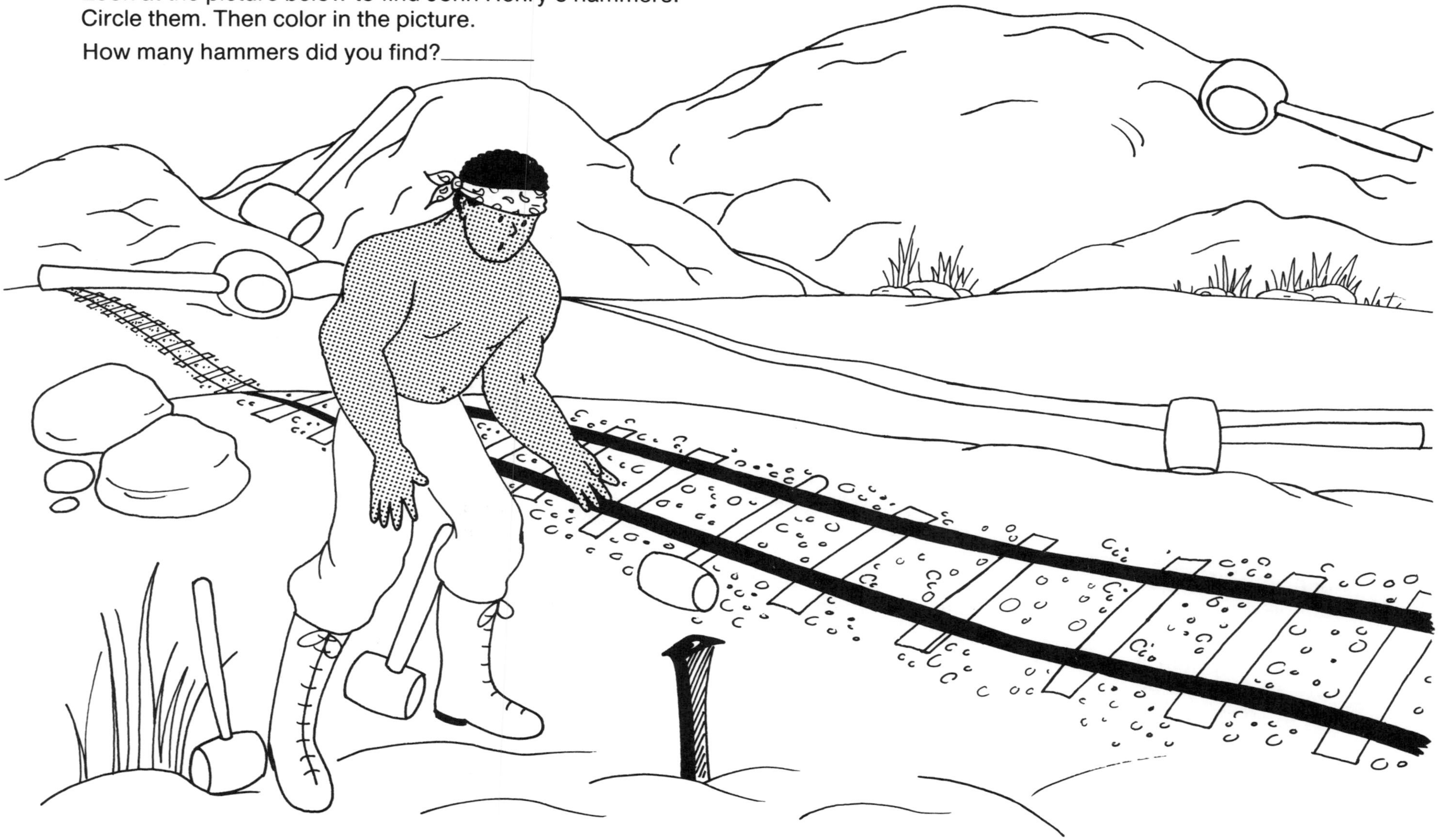

Read this story to your class. Then reproduce the worksheet on page 63 for children to complete.

Pecos Bill, the roughest, toughest cowboy that ever lived, was born in Texas. When he was two years old, he fell out of his family's covered wagon near the Pecos River as they were heading westward. His parents were so busy looking after their 13 other children that for three days nobody realized Pecos Bill was missing. By that time he had found a pack of friendly coyotes who decided to adopt him. Before long, Pecos Bill became their leader.

Pecos Bill grew up happily among the coyotes, teaching them everything he knew about humans and learning everything there was to know about coyotes. It wasn't till he was grown up that he saw another human, a fellow who happened to be a cowboy. Pecos Bill thought he himself was a coyote. It was only when the cowboy proved to him he wasn't—after all, he didn't have a tail—that he was ready to become a cowboy himself. He decided then and there to be the greatest cowboy that ever lived.

Pecos Bill's new friend taught him to talk, dress, and walk like a cowboy. Then he told Pecos Bill he would need a horse to ride. However, Pecos Bill had other ideas. "Got me an animal of my own, standing right over there," he said, pointing to a giant mountain lion that he'd fought the day before. "And this is what I'll use for a lasso." He then held up a huge rattlesnake that he had snapped into control the week before.

Well, you can imagine the expressions on the other cowboys' faces when Pecos Bill first rode into camp, sitting up straight on the giant mountain lion, twirling his rattlesnake lasso, and wiping his hot, wet brow with a handful of prickly pear cactus. Pecos Bill was made boss of the outfit right away!

Now king of the cowboys, Pecos Bill spent the next few years doing deeds cowpokes are still talking about. One of their favorite stories about him tells of the time he rode a big, black cyclone cloud. It was during the year of the great drought, when it never rained at all. The sun had been beating down on the prairie for months. The poor cattle were so thirsty that their tongues were hanging down almost to the ground. Pecos Bill knew he had to do something, so he got on his mountain lion and rode through all of Texas, galloping even into Oklahoma, until he found just what he was looking for. He saw the skies turn black. He heard thunder begin to roar. And when he heard a long, purring moan, Pecos Bill knew that the big, black cyclone was nearby.

Pecos Bill watched the huge spinning cloud come closer and closer. When it was just the right distance away, he twirled his snake lasso, which was now hundreds of miles long, three times above his head and caught the fierce cyclone by its neck.

It whirled around more fiercely than ever, but Pecos Bill held on. In the very next minute, he leaped on top of it. The cyclone seemed to snort. It tried all the tricks bucking broncos use when a roughrider tries to tame them. But Pecos Bill held on and rode the cyclone, waving his ten-gallon hat in the air and giving a coyote-yell loud enough to split any state in two.

Soon the cyclone was side-throwing, high-flying, pin-wheeling, rearing back, and doing everything it could to throw Pecos Bill. But Pecos Bill was determined to ride it out. When the cyclone showed signs of tiring, Pecos Bill edged it right over the parts of Texas that had been hit hardest by the great drought. The storming cyclone knew it was licked. Pecos Bill couldn't be thrown. So it did just what Pecos Bill wanted it to. It rained right out from under him! The rain came just in time to save thousands of cattle from dying of thirst.

Then Pecos Bill, happy and content, simply slid down to the ground on a streak of lightning and went about his ordinary business. He smiled, knowing as always that he was best at roping and fastest at running. In fact, he was king of all the cowboys that ever lived.

Discussion Questions:

1. Where was Pecos Bill born?

2. What happened to him when he was two years old?

3. What kind of animal adopted Pecos Bill?

4. Who was the first human Pecos Bill met after living with coyotes?

5. What kind of animal did Pecos Bill ride?

6. What did Pecos Bill catch with his lasso?

PECOS BILL RIDES AGAIN
Worksheet

Look at the Color Key at the bottom of the page.
Match the colors in the key with the numbers in the picture.
Then color the picture in.

Name_____

Color Key: 3=red 4=green 5=blue 6=yellow 7=brown 8=orange 9=gray

You need: *Legendary Heroes* posters included with this unit
oaktag
glue
transparent tape or pushpins

Optional: clear plastic adhesive

Steps:

1. Mount each of the *Legendary Heroes* posters on oaktag. Cover with clear plastic adhesive or laminate for durability. Display the posters on a wall or bulletin board.

2. Use the posters as visual aids, as you read the tall tales in this unit.

3. After reading each story aloud, ask children to point out examples of exaggeration in the story.

4. Explain to the children that a tall tale is based on a story that comes down from the past. Although it may be based on facts, we do not know how much of the story is true. There are often variations from one version of a tall tale to another.

Follow-up Activity:

Use sentence starters like those below to motivate children to make up their own tall tales. Younger children may tell their tall tales to the class, and older children may write their tall tales down. After creating the tall tales, children can illustrate them.

Paul Bunyan was so strong . . .
Babe was so big . . .
Davy Crockett knew so much about the forest he . . .
Davy's bear was so smart . . .
Mike Fink's keelboat once . . .
Big Mose was such a brave fire fighter, he would . . .
With his hammer, John Henry could . . .
Pecos Bill was the only cowboy that . . .